D1178249

NOH

by Daiji Maruoka
    by Tatsuo Yoshikoshi

translated by
      Don Kenny

HOIKUSHA

Contents

Cover Photo: Hashitomi Scene II
              Umewaka Rokurô

N O H

by Daiji Maruoka & Tatsuo Yoshikoshi
translated by Don Kenny

© All rights reserved. No. 15 of Hoikusha's Color Books Series. Published by Hoikusha Publishing Co., Ltd., 17-13, 1-chome, Uemachi, Higashi-ku, Osaka, 540 Japan. ISBN 4-586-54015-X. First Edition in 1969. Tenth Edition in 1982. Printed in JAPAN

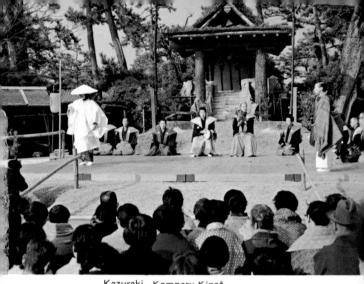

Kazuraki   Komparu Kinzô
at the Onmatsuri Festival in Nara

Noh at Nara's Onmatsuri

Annually on December 17 and 18, a festival called the Onmatsuri is held at Kasuga Wakamiya Shrine in Nara. On the first day, a special bow and arrow dance by Noh actors of the Komparu school and an old *furyû* dance by Kyôgen actors of the Ôkura school are performed beneath the ancient *yôgô* pine located on the south approach to the shrine. This is referred to as the "ceremony under the pine" (*matsu-no-shita-no-shiki*). The second day, a full formal program of five Noh and four Kyôgen is presented on a temporary low stage set up on the grass in front of the temporary shrine.

1

Okina Umewaka Rokurô

Okina

This is an ancient religious ceremony, originally performed by priests and later taken over by Noh and Kyôgen actors. It is performed as the opening number on special Noh programs. The actors participate in purification rites before the performance. All those participating in a performance of Okina, including the members of the chorus and orchestra, and the stage assistants, wear special formal costumes.

Okina is made up of three dances — Senzai, Okina, and Sanbasô. After the Senzai dance, the *shite* (the principal actor) puts on the white mask called *haku-shiki-jô* on stage just before he dances the Okina role. There is no other play in the Noh repertoire in which a mask is put in place after the actor has appeared on the stage. After the *shite* finishes his dance, he removes the mask, salutes it, returns it to its box, and leaves the stage.

Greenroom purification ceremony
before a performance of Okina

3

Okina   Kanze Motomasa

Sanbasô

After the *shite* leaves the stage, the stick drum joins in, and the rhythm of the accompaniment becomes more lively and stirring.

The Kyôgen actor appears and performs the *momi-no-dan*, a cheery dance with much stamping of feet and exclamatory shouts by the actor himself. Next he puts on the black mask called *koku-shiki-jô*, receives a cluster of gold bells from Senzai, and dances the *suzu-no-dan*, in which the bells contribute their sharp tinkle.

The Senzai and Okina dances are prayers for general good fortune and happiness, and the Sanbasô dance is a prayer for an abundant harvest.

Sanbasô   Ôkura Yatarô

Kamo Scene I Komparu Nobutaka

Waki Noh

Kamo

It is a summer evening. A priest from Harima goes to the Kamo Shrine to pray and finds a mound decorated with a white arrow near the Kamo River. He asks two women (*shite* and *tsure*), who are drawing water nearby, to tell him about the god of the Kamo Shrine.

They explain that hundreds of years ago a woman picked up a white arrow that was floating in the river, conceived, and gave birth to a thunder god. Thus the mother, the arrow, and the thunder god became the three deities of Kamo. They announce that they are the mother and the thunder god, and immediately disappear. The *shite* reappears in the second scene as the thunder god, and the *tsure* as his mother. They perform a felicitous dance of blessing.

In the photo, the stand for the arrow is in the right foreground, the *shite* is in the rear facing front, and the *tsure* is in the left foreground facing the rear.

Arashiyama

It is cherry blossom time on Mount Arashi in Kyoto. A courtier on a mission from the Emperor comes to the mountain and asks the old couple, who are gardeners there, to tell him the history of the cherry trees. The old man and woman perform a graceful dance as they tell the story. In Scene II, they appear as the god of the mountain and his attendant (as seen in the photo), and dance in celebration of spring and the cherry blossoms.

The *Ai Kyôgen* is a full-fledged monkey wedding with vocalizations representing the chattering of monkeys, in place of dialogue.

Arashiyama Scene II   Komparu Nobutaka

▲ Takasago Scene I Tomoeda Kikuo

Takasago

This is the most representative of the First Group God (*Waki Noh*) play.

A priest from Kyushu makes a pilgrimage to Takasago Bay in Harima. Spring breezes whispering through the pine trees, and the sound of the waves as they beat against the shore, join to form a lovely symphony with the soft tones of the evening bell wafting down through the mist on a mountain top nearby.

An old couple appears and they begin sweeping up the leaves, and purifying the sand on the shore. They answer with ancient poems which tell of the wedding of the pines at Sumiyoshi and Takasago. Pine trees symbolize eternal life.

The old man explains that even though separated, the hearts of a married couple should always be together. He goes on to tell of the seasons and all living things, by means of old poems.

The old man announces that he and his wife are the spirits of the pines of Sumiyoshi and Takasago. Then they board a boat and disappear into the mist over the bay.

In Scene II the god of Sumiyoshi appears and dances, announcing prosperity and long life for all mankind.

Takasago Scene II
Hōshō Hideo

9

Ema Scene II Kita Nagayo

Ema

A messenger of the Emperor is sent on a mission to Ise
Shrine. It is the first day of spring — a holiday called Setsubun.
The messenger is waiting to see the ceremony of the hanging of
the prayer plaques (*ema*) when an old couple appears. They
argue over whether to hang the black plaque for rain or the
white plaque for sunshine, and finally decide to hang both in
order to give prosperity and happiness to all mankind. Then they
announce to the messenger that they are the sun god and the
moon god, and suddenly disappear.

In Scene II, they appear as ancient gods and act out, in a
dance, the legend of the sun goddess when she hid in a cave and
was finally persuaded to reappear by the other gods.

Old Man Masks

Ko-jô (upper right), used for
   aged men
Shiwa-jô (upper left), used for
   happy old men
Aku-jô (lower), used for aged
   gods and sorrowful ghosts

Tsuru Kame   Kanze Takeo

Chikubushima Scene II   Tanaka Ikunosuke

Tsuru Kame

A court banquet is held by the Emperor to celebrate the New Year. Aristocrats from all over the realm file in to pay their respects to the Imperial family. The heavens ring with their footsteps. Gold and silver dust covers the floors of the palace, and its doors and staircases are decked with myriad jewels. A red-crested crane alights in the garden and a tortoise emerges from the water of the lake. The crane (*tsuru*) and the tortoise (*kame*) are traditional symbols of happiness and longevity. They dance for the court, and the Emperor joins them.

This is the only one-scene play among those of the First Group God (*Waki Noh*) plays. In the Kita school it is called *Gekkyûden*.

Chikubushima

It is March. A courtier is sent to Lake Biwa on a mission from the Emperor. A fisherman and a woman diver take him to Chikubu Island in their boat.

The woman reveals that she is Benten, the goddess of good fortune, and disappears into the shrine. The fisherman announces, "I am the Master of the Lake," and dives into the water.

In Scene II, the goddess Benten appears in all her glory, and the dragon god emerges from the lake. They perform a felicitous dance of blessing.

Kiyotsune   Kita Roppeita

Shura Mono
Kiyotsune

This is an unusual Second Group Ghost (*Shura Mono*) play, as it tells of love as well as combat.

The former brilliance of the Heike Clan dims as they lose battle after battle. The white flag of the Genji Clan spreads across the face of the land.

Kiyotsune, the Heike warrior, has made a fatal decision. He stands on the prow of the boat in the moonlight, and plays his farewell to the world on his favorite flute. He leaps into the waters of the lake and intones a Buddhist prayer as he sinks out of sight.

A retainer takes a lock of Kiyotsune's hair to his wife and announces the sad news. She is stricken with grief at the loss of her beloved husband.

That night Kiyotsune appears to his wife in a dream and comforts her, accompanied by the sad tones of a flute.

Atsumori

Kumagai Naozane killed Atsumori, a Young Heike warrior, in the battle of Ichinotani. In remorse, he took the name Rensei, and became a priest to pray for Atsumori's soul. He returns to the sight of the battle and hears the sound of a flute. He is standing, lost in reverie, when a group of woodcutters appears. One of the woodcutters stays behind, and Rensei questions him. He reveals that he is related to Atsumori, and immediately disappears.

Rensei begins a night-long vigil of prayer. Atsumori's ghost appears, tells of the happy life he had led, and plays on the flute that he was carrying when he died. He forgives Rensei and asks him to continue praying for his soul.

Atsumori Scene I   Kanze Shizuo

Yashima
Scene II
Umewaka
Rokurō

Yashima

It is a spring night at Yashima. An old fisherman tells a
wandering priest the story of the battle fought there many years
before. In Scene II, the fisherman appears in his true form, as
the ghost of Yoshitsune, the Genji general, tells of his tortures
in hell, and requests that the priest pray for his soul.

16

Tadanori

A wandering priest questions a woodcutter about a beautiful cherry tree in Suma. The woodcutter explains that it was planted in memory of Tadanori, the warrior-poet, who was slain in battle on the same spot. The priest stays under the tree to pray for Tadanori's soul.

The ghost of Tadanori appears to the priest and tells him that the man who killed him took a poem that he had written just before he died, and had it published. His soul has found no rest because the poem was published without its author's name, since Tadanori had neglected to announce his name to his enemy.

Tadanori
Scene II
Awaya
Kikuo

Yorimasa Scene II
Kanze Yoshiyuki

Yorimasa

An old man guides a wandering priest around the sights of Uji. He explains that the fan-shaped lawn of the Byôdô-in was planted as a memorial to Yorimasa, a warrior-poet, who had disembowled himself on the same spot after composing a poem telling of his defeat in battle. He announces that this is the anniversary of Yorimasa's death, and immediately disappears.

The priest begins to pray for Yorimasa's soul. The ghost of Yorimasa appears, tells of his last battle, his defeat, and his death. He thanks the priest for his prayers.

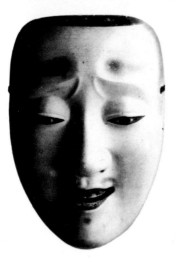

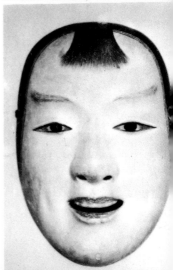

Male Masks

Jidô (upper right), used for
demigods and young men
Chûjô (upper left), used for
adult aristocrats
Kasshiki (lower), used for
young lay-priests

Sanemori Scene II Honda Hideo

Sanemori

Yugyô, a Buddhist priest, wanders around the edge of a certain pond every day mumbling sutras to himself. One day an old man appears to him, and explains that he is the ghost of Sanemori, a warrior, whose head had been severed from his body and washed in this very pond two hundred years before.

Late that night, Yugyô is praying for Sanemori's soul when his ghost appears in full battle dress, and tells how he concealed his age by dyeing his beard and hair black, in order to be allowed to fight alongside the young warriors. He thanks Yugyô for his prayers.

Tomoe

A young woman stops a wandering priest on Awazu Plain near Lake Biwa and asks him to perform a memorial service, and disappears as suddenly as she had come.

The young woman appears during the prayers in her true form, as the ghost of Tomoe, a female warrior. Tomoe had accompanied her husband into battle to be near him at all times, but she had not been able to die with him. She thanks the priest for his prayers.

This is the only Second Group Ghost (*Shura Mono*) play in which the *shite* is a woman.

Tomoe Scene II
Hôshô Kurô

Orchestra playing the prelude in the greenroom

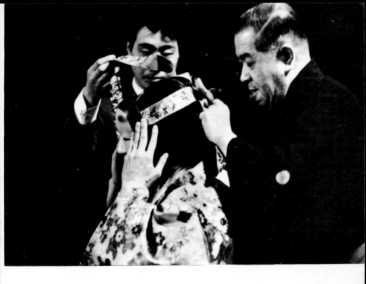

Izutsu Scene I   Matsumoto Kenzô

23

Katsura Mono

Izutsu

A wandering priest arrives at Ariwara Temple on his tour of worship at the main temples of Nara. Hundreds of years before, Ariwara Narihira, the poet-aristocrat and grandson of the Emperor, had lived here with his wife, the daughter of Ki Aritsune.

The priest begins to pray for the repose of their souls. It is autumn. The sun sets and the breezes whisper through the boughs of the pine trees. The moon moves toward the west and seems to rest on the eaves of the temple.

A young girl appears and begins praying earnestly. The priest wonders why a young girl would come alone to such a lonely temple at night. Could she be someone who has committed some grave sin and is now seeking enlightenment? Perhaps she is the ghost of someone who was attached in some way to this place in her lifetime.

The girl goes to a wooden well (*izutsu*) in the temple grounds and begins drawing water. She waters the flowers on a nearby grave.

Izutsu Scene I
Kita Nagayo
The shite begins his progress down the bridge-like hashi-gakari

25

In answer to the priest's questions, she explains that the temple had been built by Narihira, and that he now lies in this grave. He was the grandson of Emperor Heizei, who had bestowed the family name Ariwara on him and his brother Yukihira. But it had all happened so many years ago.

The priest asks why a young girl like herself should still be offering prayers in memory of a man who had lived such a long time ago. The girl answers vaguely, "Even in the *Tales of Ise*, which was written a long time ago, Narihira is mentioned as a man of the long distant past."

The pine tree nearby is gnarled with age, weeds grow in profusion all around, and the reeds around the grave are drenched with dew.

The girl goes to the well once more, and murmurs, "How I long for the olden days." She goes on to tell how Narihira fell in love with another girl and went to visit her often. The daughter of Ki Aritsune poured her heart into poems describing her sadness. She sincerely hoped no harm would come to her husband as he made his way through the night to his new-found love.

The girl wanders off, and a villager comes by. The priest questions him and he relates more of the story of Narihira.

Izutsu Interval   Ôkura Yatarô

Izutsu Scene I   Kanze Hisao

When Narihira and the daughter of Ki Aritsune were children,
their families had lived in this very place, next door to each
other. This well was in front of their houses. The two children
used to play together, resting their sleeves upon the wooden
curb of the well. They would press close to each other and watch
the reflection of their faces in the water of the well. In time,
they grew up, and became shy of playing such childish games.
They saw each other less and less.

One day Narihira sent her a love poem which read, "I leaned on the well, and when I saw my face in the water, I realized that you too must have grown. I recalled how we used to compare our height when we were children." She sent her reply saying, "I wonder who could possibly be compared with you and be found worthy to be your wife."

At this point the girl reappears and interrupts saying, "I am that daughter of Aritsune. Narihira and I became husband and wife when I was only nineteen." Then she disappears once more into the shadows near the well.

The priest decides to spend the night here, in prayer for rest for her soul.

The girl appears to the priest in a dream. She is dressed in Narihira's cloak and hat. She announces that she will dance as Narihira danced.

The gentle light of the moon is clear and bright. As she dances, she recalls one of Narihira's poems, "The moon may change. This spring is not the same as that spring. But I am as I was before." How long it is since these words were spoken. She approaches the well and gazes at her reflection upon the water. There she sees, not her own face, but the face of her beloved Narihira. She fades away, with a sigh of yearning for the past, like the wilting of a beautiful flower. The bell of the temple announces the dawn.

Izutsu Scene II   Kita Nagayo ▶

Tôboku

A priest arrives in Kyoto. He is lost in wonder gazing at the plum blossoms at Tôboku Temple.

A graceful peasant girl appears, and tells him that the trees were planted many years before by Izumi Shikibu, the famed Heian period poetess.

The rays of the evening sun deepen the color of the delicate pink-white plum blossoms. As the shadows deepen, the girl reveals that she is the spirit of the plum blossom, and disappears.

The priest begins praying. The girl reappears in her true form, as the dazzlingly beautiful spirit, and says, "Your prayer is from the Lotus Sutra. Lord Fujiwara Michinaga often repeated the same words here. Through his prayers, these plum trees of Tôboku Temple have been designated as sacred." She performs a lovely dance as she tells this story.

Tôboku Scene II
Kanze Tetsunojô

Kazuraki

A warrior-priest (*yamabushi*) and his attendants are on their way to climb Mount Kazuraki. They are caught in a sudden snow storm. A peasant girl calls to them, offering shelter from the storm. Covered with snow, they make their way to the cottage in the valley. She makes them comfortable in front of a warm fire.

The priests' clothes are dried and they begin their early morning prayers. The girl asks for prayers on her behalf, and disappears.

She reappears in her true form, as the goddess of Mount Kazuraki. Her costume is decorated in vines and ivy. She performs a graceful dance in gratitude for their prayers.
their prayers.

Kazuraki Scene I
Kanai Akira

Matsukaze   Umemura Heishirô

Yuya   Shite: Inoue Kitarô ▶
Waki: Teshima Jûrô

Matsukaze

A wandering priest arrives at Suma Bay. Two girls appear to gather salt. They reveal to him that they are the ghosts of Matsukaze and Murasame, two sisters who were loved by Yukihira, the poet-aristocrat, when he was exiled to this place.

Matsukaze dons Yukihira's hat and robe, which he had left them as a memento. She dances as she tells of her memories. Dawn breaks, and the priest hears nothing but the murmur of the wind in the pines.

Yuya

It is spring. Yuya, Munemori's mistress, receives word that her mother who lives in the east is seriously ill. She requests permission to visit her mother, but Munemori forces her to accompany him on a flower viewing party at Kiyomizu Temple. She is dancing under the cherry blossoms when there is a sudden shower. Cherry blossoms fall in the rain, and Yuya composes a poem which reads, "What can I do? Leaving the capital in spring is sad, but even sadder would be the loss of the flower I love in the east." Munemori is moved and gives her permission to go to her mother.

Yugyô Yanagi Scene II   Yamaguchi Naotomo

Yugyô Yanagi

It is autumn. Priest Yugyô is guided to an ancient willow tree by an old villager. The villager tells the history of the tree, and later appears as the willow spirit and dances until dawn in gratitude for the priest's prayers.

Saigyô Zakura

It is spring. A group of people come to enjoy the blossoms of a cherry tree near the priest-poet Saigyô's hermitage. He writes a poem in which he blames the cherry tree for the intrusion. That night, the spirit of the cherry tree appears to Saigyô, denies that it was at fault, and dances in celebration of spring, until the morning sun begins to tint the horizon.

34

Saigyô Zakura   Hashioka Kyûtarô

Eguchi

A priest arrives at Eguchi, a port town, where a prostitute named Eguchi-no-Kimi lies buried. He recites a poem which had been composed by Saigyô about Eguchi-no-Kimi. A woman appears, answers the poem, and reveals that she is the ghost of Eguchi-no-Kimi.

The priest and his attendants are praying for her soul when several pleasure boats appear on the surface of the water. They are filled with women, singing and dancing. Among them is Eguchi-no-Kimi. To a spring flower, full bloom means coming death. The sparkle of morning dew forcasts the fading of maple leaves in autumn.

Eguchi-no-Kimi is suddenly transformed into the compassionate goddess Fugen. The boat becomes a white elephant. The goddess rides the elephant up into white clouds, which emit brilliant rays of light.

Eguchi Scene II
Shite: Kanze Tetsunojô
Tsure: Fuji Tokuzô and
  Endô Rokurô

Yôkihi

The T'ang Emperor Hsuau Tsuug of China is stricken with grief at the death of his beloved consort Yôkihi. He sends a Taoist priest to search for her soul to the ends of the earth.

The priest finds her on Mount Hôrai in the island paradise. They speak of the Emperor. The priest asks her for some token for the Emperor, to prove that this is really Yôkihi. She reveals a secret promise that she and the Emperor had made when she was alive. "If we meet next in the heavens, we pray to be a pair of doves, ever flying wing to wing; if we meet again on earth, we pray to become twin trees with branches eternally entwined around each other."

Yôkihi weeps tears of joy for the past and for the Emperor's continuing love for her. She dances, telling of the exquisite nights of pleasure she had enjoyed with the Emperor when she was alive.

Yôkihi Scene II
Umewaka Rokurô

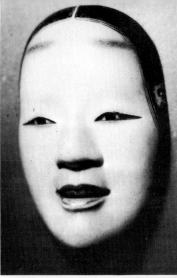

Female Masks

Waka-onna (upper right),
   used for young women
Fukai (upper left), used
   for middle-aged women
Zô-onna (lower), used for
   angels and goddesses

Ohara Gokô

It is the season when yellow roses bloom and nightingales sing. Retired Emperor Goshirakawa journeys to Jakkô Temple in Ohara to visit the nun Kenreimon, who is living there in meditation. When he arrives, she has gone to pick flowers in the hills behind the temple.

She is surprised to see Emperor Goshirakawa when she returns, apologizes for her absence, and prepares to entertain him.

Goshirakawa questions Kenreimon, and she retells the story of the defeat at the battle of Dan-no-ura. She had jumped into the sea with her infant son, the Emperor Antoku, to avoid capture by the enemy Minamoto Clan. Emperor Antoku had drowned, but she had been rescued, after which she became a nun to pray for her son's soul.

As the day comes to a close, Emperor Goshirakawa says farewell and begins his journey home. Kenreimon stands watching at the door of her hut long after the Emperor's entourage has disappeared from sight.

Ohara Gokô Scene II
Kanze Yoshiyuki

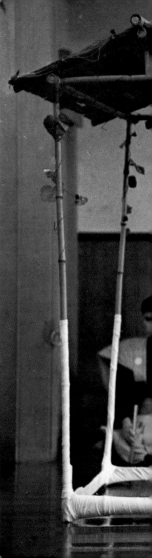

Kakitsubata Scene II
Umewaka Masatoshi

Kakitsubata

Yatsuhashi in Mikawa is famous for its beautiful irises (*kakitsubata*). A wandering priest arrives when the flowers are in full bloom. He meets a village girl who recites the poem which is an anagram on the name Kakitsubata, and was written by Narihira, the Heian period poet-aristocrat.

The girl invites the priest to spend the night at her hut. Later she appears before him wearing Narihira's hat and cloak. She reveals that she is the spirit of the iris, and dances in gratitude to Narihira for immortalizing the iris in his beautiful poem.

Uneme

It is March at the Sarusawa Pond in Nara. A village girl guides a traveling priest to the pond. She tells the story of Uneme, who had been a consort of the Emperor many years ago. The Emperor had a change of heart, and Uneme, broken hearted, threw herself into this very pond and died. She announces that she is the ghost of Uneme, and disappears into the water of the pond.

The waves lap the shore while the priest intones prayers of invocation. Uneme's ghost appears on the surface of the water, and tells of her happy life at court in a delicately beautiful dance.

Uneme Scene II Kanze Hisao

Hagoromo   Kanze Motomasa

Nonomiya Scene II   Takahashi Susumu

Hagoromo

A fisherman finds a beautiful feather robe (*hagoromo*) hanging on the branches of a pine tree on the beach at Matsubara in Miho. An angel appears and pleads tearfully that he return the robe to her, for she cannot make her way back to heaven without it. He finally consents and she dances in gratitude as she flies heavenward.

Nonomiya

Prince Genji's mistress Lady Rokujô's ghost haunts a small hut called Nonomiya on the bleak plains at Sagano. She dances for a wandering priest, telling him the story of a quarrel she had had over the position of her carriage at the Kamo festival with Lady Aoi, Genji's legal wife.

45

Teika

The scene is an ancient dwelling called Shigure-no-Chin where the poet-aristocrat Fujiwara Teika lived many years ago.

A woman guides a wandering priest to a grave in the garden. It is the grave of Princess Shokushi who died after a very short love affair with Teika. Teika had been so in love with Princess Shokushi that his spirit became a creeper-vine after his death, and twined himself firmly around the princess' tombstone. The woman reveals that she is the spirit of Princess Shokushi, and disappears into the tomb.

The priest recites prayers of invocation, and the emaciated figure of the princess appears. Teika's love, in the form of the vine, allows her soul no rest.

Teika Scene II
Kondō Kenzō

46

Obasute Scene II   Kanze Tetsunojô

Obasute

It is the night of August 15th, and the full moon shines in all its glory. Men from the capital arrive at Mount Obasute to enjoy the famous moon-lit view.

A woman approaches, and tells them of an old woman whose son abandoned her to die, according to the ancient custom of the area, in a grove of judas trees nearby.

The woman disappears and before long an old woman appears, dancing in the soft, gentle light of the moon, telling of past happiness, and the bliss which prayers can bring.

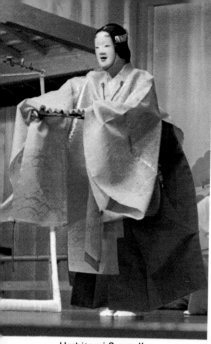

Hashitomi Scene II
Umewaka Manzaburô

Hashitomi

It is summer. The priest of Unrin Temple is in meditation. A young woman comes every day to offer flowers. The priest suspects that she is the ghost of Yûgao, mistress of Prince Genji.

The priest goes to Yûgao's old residence, and finds the lawn covered with weeds and moonflowers (*yûgao*). A girl beckons to him from an open window-wicket (*hashitomi*), and draws him into the world of the past.

Futari Shizuka

It is January. A woman goes to gather herbs to offer at the Katsute Shrine. She looks up while gathering the herbs and sees the ghost of Princess Shizuka, Yoshitsune's mistress.

The woman runs to tell a priest what she has seen. She becomes possessed by the ghost, dons a costume once worn by Shizuka, and begins to dance. Shizuka's ghost appears once more, and dances with the bewitched woman.

Futari Shizuka Scene II ▶
Shite: Hashioka Kyûma, Tsure: Kanze Hisao

Zatsu Noh

Aoi-no-ue

The *waki* takes his place on the stage costumed to play the role of a soothe sayer. A brocade *kimono* is placed down stage center to represent Lady Aoi, prince Genji's legal wife, who is being torture by an unknown illness.

The soothsayer is searching for the cause of the sickness. The spirit of Lady Rokujô, Genji's mistress, reveals itself through the lips of the soothe sayer, and explains that it has possessed Lady Aoi's body because of jealousy. Lady Aoi's servants had insulted Lady Rokujô at the Kamo Festival.

Aoi-no-ue Scene II
Shite: Sakurama Ryûma, Waki: Matsumoto Kenzô

Aoi-no-ue Scene I   Kanze Kasetsu

A priest is sent for to exorcise the spirit. The spirit appears in its true form, as a ferocious demon with horns, the very embodiment of feminine jealousy. A great struggle ensues, which ends with victory for the priest, and renewed health for Lady Aoi.

Dōjōji Scene I　Komparu Nobutaka

Dôjôji

The dedication ceremony is being held for the new bell at Dôjô Temple. A beautiful *Shirabyôshi* dancer comes to dance for the celebration. During her dance she comes near the bell, jumps up inside it, and pulls it down. The priests realize that she is the same girl who chased her lover into the original bell and melted it with her frustrated fury.

The priests finally succeed in lifting the bell once more, only to be confronted by a ferocious serpent demon — the embodiment of the girl's frustration and jealousy.

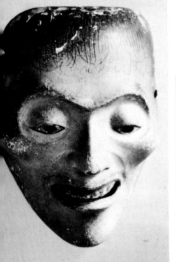

Masks

Deigan (upper right), used for
jealous women
Han'nya (upper left), used for
spirits of jealous women
Kawazu (lower), used for spirits
of drowned men

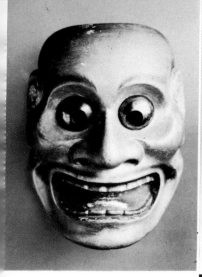

Ko-beshimi (upper right), used
for sorrowful demons
Ô-tobide (upper left), used for
violent demons
Shishi-guchi (lower), used for
the spirit of a lion

Fujito

Sasaki Moritsuna was awarded Kojima as his fief in return for successfully crossing the Fujito Straits, and conquering the Heike army. He announces that he will grant an audience to any subject who wishes to make a petition.

An old woman charges Moritsuna with the murder of her innocent twenty year old son. At first he denies any knowledge of the matter, but seeing the great grief of the mother, he admits his crime. The son had guided Moritsuna and his army across the straits. Since the boy was a subject of enemy territory, Moritsuna had murdered him to keep the crossing secret.

Moritsuna expresses his regrets, and offers prayers for the soul of the dead boy. The spirit of the boy appears, describes his death, and expresses deep gratitude for the prayers which have enabled him to attain salvation.

Fujito Scene I
Shite: Kanze Hisao
Waki: Matsumoto Kenzô

Kayoi Komachi

It is summer. A priest has come to Yase to meditate. Every day a young woman comes and presents him with offerings of wood and fruit. One day he asks who she is. She replies, "I am Komachi from Ichiharano," and disappears.

The priest preceives that she is the spirit of the beautiful poetess of long ago. He goes to Komachi's grave in Ichiharano and offers incense and prayers. Komachi's ghost appears and joyfully expresses gratitude. Behind Komachi appears the ghost of a man who tells his sad story. He is Fukakusa to whom Komachi promised her love if he would visit her every night for one hundred nights. Fukakusa visited her ninety-nine times, but died before his visit the next day. His unrequited love has kept his soul from eternal rest.

Kayoi Komachi
Umewaka Naoyoshi

◀ Fujito Scene II
Umewaka Minoru

Koi-no-Omoni

An elderly palace gardener fell in love with a court lady. In jest, she has a heavy stone wrapped in brocade and placed in the garden. She taunts the gardener, telling him that if he will carry the package around the garden, she will give him her love.

The gardener exhausts himself trying to lift the stone, and dies, his heart full of resentment and anger.

The lady regrets her frivolous deed, and goes to ask forgiveness at his grave. The spirit of the old gardener appears, and berates her for her heartlessness, but upon seeing her sincere regret, forgives her and leaves her in peace, promising to protect her from all harm.

Koi-no-Omoni Scene I   Kanze Yoshiyuki

Kinuta Scene I   Honda Hideo

Kinuta

The lord of Ashiya in Kyushu has been in the capital on business for three years. He sends Yûgiri, a maid-servant, to comfort his wife and assure her that he will return by the end of the year.

In the moon light on an autumn evening, Yûgiri and the wife pound cloth together on a fulling board (*Kinuta*). The wife wonders if the pounding of the cloth on the board and of her lonely heart in her breast can be heard by her husband.

Another servant brings news that the Lord will not be able to return as he promised. The lonely wife takes ill and dies.

The husband returns home, and discovers his loss. He has the spirit of his wife recalled. She tells of her tortures in hell because of her loneliness and bitterness. The husband chants prayers to put her soul to rest.

Kinuta Scene II　Tomoeda Kikuo

Utou

A wandering priest on his way down a mountain meets an old man who begs the priest to visit his home. He explains that he is the ghost of a bird hunter who died without saying farewell to his wife. He gives the priest his rush hat, his feathered apron, and a sleeve of a kimono to give to his wife to prove to her that the priest had really met her husband, the dead hunter.

The priest agrees, goes to the hunter's home, and offers an invocation. The hunter's ghost appears to his family, but he cannot come close to them. He tells of his tortures in hell which are in retribution for taking the lives of birds called *utou* when he was on earth.

Utou Scene I Nagashima Seiji

Utou Scene II
Umewaka
 Naoyoshi

Makura Jidô

An Emperor of ancient China sends an envoy to search for the elixir of life.

The envoy comes to a waterfall where he meets a youthful demi-god (*jidô*) who explains that it is he who makes the elixir by writing a magic formula on chrysanthemum leaves which grow in profusion in the area. He also reveals that he had been exiled to this place when he stepped across the Emperor's pillow (*makura*) seven hundred years ago. The demi-god gives the envoy some of the precious elixir and dances and sings in his honor.

Makura Jidô
Kongô Iwao

65

Sotoba Komachi　Asami Shinken

Sotoba Komachi

On their way to the capital, a group of priests come across an old beggar woman sitting on a wooden grave marker (*sotoba*). They try to chase her away, admonishing her with scriptures. She reproaches them with even more learned quotations from scripture. The priests are surprised and bow low in apology. She reveals that she is Ono-no Komachi, the once beautiful and famous poetess.

Suddenly she is seized by the ghost of Fukakusa, the suitor who she had forced to visit her one hundred nights to gain her love (see *Kayoi Komachi*). She reenacts his miserable visits and subsequent death, in a dance. The ghost finally leaves her, and she becomes calm once more.

Kantan
Noguchi Yoshihisa

Kantan

Rosei, a Chinese youth, is weary of life and sets out on a pilgrimage to Mount Yôhi to gain enlightenment. He stops to spend the night at a village called Kantan. He is given a magic pillow to sleep on.

He dreams that he is appointed Emperor. He is borne to a richly decorated palace on a sedan chair. The courtyards are strewn with gold and silver dust, and the courtiers are brilliantly dressed in gorgeous attire. The throne room is piled high with heaps of gifts for the new Emperor.

Rosei reigns for fifty years, surrounded by happiness and prosperity. On his fiftieth anniversary, he drinks the wine of eternal life, and he dances with his courtiers, in celebration.

The proprietress of the inn in Kantan wakes Rosei to serve him rice with chestnuts, upon which he realizes that life is like a momentary dream. He resolves to give up any further travel, and to return home to spend the rest of his days in quiet meditation.

Jinen Koji   Kita Minoru

Yoroboshi

A blind youth named Yoroboshi begs on the stairs of Shitennô Temple. He spreads his sleeves to receive alms, but catches falling plum blossoms instead. Though he cannot see, he can smell their beauty. He realizes that if the eyes of the soul are open, one can live in spiritual happiness. He dances for joy at his new found knowledge.

His father who had disowned him is present. He is moved by the boy's faith, and leads him back home.

Yoroboshi   Kanze Shizuo

Jinen Koji

Jinen, a young lay priest, is preaching at Unkô Temple when a small girl appears, and presents him with a robe. A note is attached which explains that the girl sold herself into slavery so that she could buy the robe in order to have an invocation service performed for her dead parents.

Jinen Koji calls to the boatman

The slave dealers come and drag the girl away. Jinen runs after them with the robe around his shoulders. He catches up with them just as they are ready to set out from Ôtsu by boat. He leaps into the boat just as it pulls away from shore. He tries to exchange the robe, which is now soiled, for the girl. The slave dealers laugh at him, and beat the girl severely.

Jinen Koji boards the boat

The slave dealers finally agree to release the girl when Jinen agrees to entertain them with songs and dances. Jinen gives the girl her freedom, and sends her on her way back to the capital.

Jinen Koji   beats on the gunwales of the boat

Sumidagawa

A deranged mother searches for her lost child all the way from Kyoto to the banks of the Sumida River in Edo (present Tokyo). She sees a group of people on the opposite shore holding a memorial service in front of a grave. She crosses the river and questions the people. They explain that a boy from the capital named Umewaka is buried there. She realizes her son is dead, and begins praying in front of the grave. The ghost of Umewaka appears and comforts his mother until dawn.

Sumidagawa
Shite: Umewaka
    Manzaburô
Waki: Hôshô Yaichi

Mitsuyama
Scene II
Shite: Nomura
Ransaku (back)
Tsure:
Takahashi Isamu

Mitsuyama

Three famous mountains stand in Yamato. Once a man lived on Mount Kaku and had a mistress on both Mount Miminashi and Mount Unebi. One of the girls drowned herself in a lake in despair.

Many years later a priest comes to pray for the girl's soul. The ghosts of both girls appear and request prayers.

73

Tenko Scene II
Umewaka Yasuyuki

Tenko

Almost two thousand years ago in China, a woman dreamed that a wonderful drum fell from heaven, on the night that she conceived. She bore a son and named him Tenko (literally, "heavenly drum"). A few years later a drum did fall from the heavens. Whenever Tenko beat upon it, it produced beautiful music.

The Emperor demanded the drum, but the boy took it to the mountains and hid. He was captured and executed by drowning.

The drum was taken to the Emperor, but it made no sound. Tenko's father was called to the palace, and when he touched the drum, it resounded beautifully. The Emperor grants the father a memorial service for his dead son as a reward.

It is an autumn night. The moon beams flow softly, the waves gently ripple, and the sky is bright with stars. Tenko's ghost appears and dances in gratitude for the prayers.

Sakuragawa

A boy named Sakura from Hyûga sold himself into slavery in order to relieve his mother's poverty. He sent the money to his mother by messenger, and was taken far away by the slave trader. The mother became deranged with sorrow, and began to wander in search of her son.

It is spring three years later. The boy has become an acolyte at Isobe Temple in Hitachi. He accompanies the older priests on a cherry blossom viewing party near the Sakura River. The mother has wandered to the same spot, and is dipping cherry (*sakura*) petals off the surface of the water in a frenzied dance. Sakura and his mother recognize each other, the priests give the boy his freedom, and mother and son promise to dedicate their lives to prayer and meditation in gratitude.

Sakuragawa Scene II
Matsumoto Shigeo

Hanjo

Lord Yoshida finds that his mistress Hanako has been sent away from home, and no one knows her whereabouts. He goes to Kamo Shrine to pray and finds her there, dancing with a fan he had given her. They are happily reunited.

Hibariyama

Toyonari had disowned his daughter and sent her away with her nurse. They are now living on Mt. Hibari, and the nurse sells flowers in a nearby village to keep them alive. Toyonari comes to the area to hunt. He meets the old nurse, finds that his reason for disowning his daughter was unfounded in fact, and regrets his rash action. Father and daughter are happily reunited.

Hanjo Scene II
Umewaka Rokurô

Semimaru

The Emperor banishes his two children Prince Semimaru and Princess Sakagami because Semimaru is blind and Sakagami has a strange affliction in which her hair stands on end. The two meet years later on Mount Ôsaka, and comfort each other for a time.

Hibariyama Scene II Kihara Yasuo

Semimaru Shite: Kanze Hisao, Waki: Yamamoto Naoyoshi

Miidera

A mother, who is distracted at the disappearance of her son, entreats the goddess of Kiyomizu Temple to help her find him. She is told in a dream to visit Mii Temple.

It is the night of the full moon, and the priests are enjoying the view at Mii Temple. The son Senmitsu is with them.

The mother, now deranged with grief, reaches the temple grounds, climbs the tower, and strikes the bell. The priests come to see who is causing the disturbance. Mother and son recognize each other and are happily reunited.

Miidera Scene II
Sakurama Ryûma

Kagekiyo Komparu Hachijô

Kagekiyo

Kagekiyo, once a brave Heike warrior, was finally taken prisoner and exiled to Hyûga. He is now a blind old beggar whose life depends on the generosity of the villagers.

His daughter, whom he has never met, hears of his plight, searches, and finally finds him. At first he denies that he is Kagekiyo out of shame for his destitute condition, but he finally succumbs to his daughter's sincere concern. Father and daughter weep tears of joy, and he tells her tales of the battles he fought in days gone by.

Ataka

Yoshitsune and his followers are traveling disguised as warrior-priests in an attempt to escape the jealous wrath of his brother Yoritomo.

They reach the barrier station at Ataka. Togashi, the inspector, knows who they are, but is so moved by Yoshitsune's retainer Benkei's show of loyalty to his master, that he lets them pass through the gate.

Togashi follows them a short distance and offers them wine. Benkei dances in joy and gratitude.

Ataka   Shite: Umewaka Rokurô, Waki: Mori Shigeyoshi

Shunkan

Shunkan, a priest from Hôshô Temple, and his two companions were exiled to uninhabited Kikai Island in Kyûshû for plotting to overthrow the Heike government. After several years pass, the Empress declares a general amnesty upon the birth of a new crown prince. An emissary is sent with the pardons, but Shunkan's name is not on the list. He clings to his friends and begs the emissary to allow him to return with them but is refused. As the boat puts out to sea, Shunkan holds fast to the hawser, but it is wrenched from his hands and the boat sails out of sight. Shunkan is left to die alone.

Shunkan   Umewaka Masatoshi

Kosode Soga Shite: Sakurama Michio (left)
Waki: Honda Hideo (right)

Kosode Soga

The Soga brothers have decided to carry
out their vendetta against their father's mur-
derer on a royal hunting party held by the
Kamakura Shôgun Yoritomo. They visit their
mother to inform her of their plan. The mother
refuses to see Gorô, the younger of the two,
because he broke his promise to become a
priest. Jûrô pleads with his mother, explaining
the reasons for Gorô's behavior and their plan
for revenge. She finally relents and the three
weep tears of joy. The brothers perform a lively
unison dance in celebration and as a final
farewell to their mother.

83

Rôtaiko Takase Sumiyuki

Rôtaiko

The Lord of Matsuura in Kyûshû throws his subject Seiji into prison for killing a friend in a brawl. Seiji escapes and his wife is brought in for questioning. She is hysterical with fear and anxiety. She doesn't know where her beloved husband is, and is greatly concerned for his welfare. The Lord releases her, but she refuses to leave the cell her husband had been in. She beats on the prison drum (rôtaiko), and declares that she feels close to her doomed husband in this cell. Moved to compassion, the Lord grants her an unconditional pardon for both herself and her husband.

Kichiku Mono

Ama

Minister Fusazaki learns that his mother was a diver from Shido Bay in Shikoku. He goes there to offer prayers for her soul.

When he arrives at the bay, he meets a woman who tells him the story of three treasures which had been sent from the Chinese Emperor. Two had arrived safely, but the third was lost in this very bay. The former Minister, Fusazaki's father, fell

Ama Scene II   Uzawa Masashi

in love with a girl diver. They had a son, and he promised her that her son would become the next minister if she would rescue the precious jewel. She dived to the bottom of the sea, and found the jewel gaurded by a ferocious dragon. She fought with the dragon and gained possession of the jewel by cutting her own breast open and hiding it inside. She died as she presented the jewel to the Minister.

Fusazaki realizes that the diver in the story was his mother. He holds a memorial service for her. Her ghost appears as a dragon woman, and dances in gratitude and joy.

Kokaji

Munechika, the famous swordsmith (*kokaji*), is ordered to make a sword for the Emperor. He goes to Inari Shrine and prays for aid. A demi-god appears, describes famous ancient swords of Japan and China, and assures him of the needed assistance. Munechika returns home, and when he begins work on the sword, the fox god Inari himself appears, and together they forge a fine sword.

Kurama Tengu

It is cherry blossom time on Mount Kurama. Ushiwaka (later Yoshitsune) is among a group of acolytes who come to view the flowers. A fierce looking warrior-priest joins them. All flee in fear except Ushiwaka. The priest explains that he is the chief goblin (*tengu*) of the mountain, and promises that he will teach the young Ushiwaka all the secrets of the martial arts.

Kurama Tengu Scene II   Shite: Kanze Yoshiyuki
Kokata: Kanze Keiyû

Kokaji Scene II   Yamaguchi Kôtoku

Funa Benkei Scene II
Shite: Umewaka Kagefusa

Kokata: Sekine Yoshito

Tôru Scene II
Teshima Yazaemon

Tôru

A priest meets an old man carrying salt pails in the center of Kyoto. When the priest questions him, the old man answers that Minamoto Tôru once built a mansion in the same area, in the garden of which he constructed a complete replica of Shiogama Bay in northern Japan. He is carrying salt water to the salt drying pans in this garden. The old man relates many tales of the former glory of the minister Tôru. Finally as the moon rises he goes on his way.

The priest is preparing to bed down for the night when the area becomes as bright as day. The ghost of Minamoto Tôru, dressed in all his former glory, approaches across the lake in his garden and dances for the priest telling of his happy life which is now far in the past.

Yamanba

A professional dancer has become famous for her song and dance entitled "Devil Woman of the Mountains" (*Yamanba*).

She decides to go on a pilgrimage to Zenkô Temple. The road is very steep and she stops to rest. Suddenly it becomes very dark. A woman appears and offers the dancer a rest in her cottage. When they reach the cottage, the woman praises the dancer for her famous skills, and disappears.

Soon the woman reappears in her true form, as the real devil woman. She dances and sings for the bewildered dancer, extolling nature and the four seasons.

Yamanba Scene II   Awaya Shintarô

91

Shôjô

A wine seller goes to the shore to sell wine. A child-faced sprite (*shôjô*) appears and requests a drink. The wine seller gives him all the wine he wants. The sprite rewards him by dancing and finally by bewitching his wine jug so that it will always be full.

Shôjô Midare
Kanze Motoaki

Kurozuka

An old woman lives alone in a hut on the bleak Adachi Plain. Every night she spins till dawn lamenting the transience of the world and the sinfulness of mankind. A priest happens by, and she warns him not to look inside her hut while she is gone to gather fire wood. He breaks his promise. The hut is filled with human bones. The old woman appears in her true form, as a witch, and attacks the priest.

Kurozuka Scene II Awaya Kikuo 93

Sagi

The Emperor visits the Shinsen Gardens. He sees a beautiful white heron (*sagi*) resting on the other side of the lake, and orders a courtier to capture it. When the courtier approaches, the heron flies away. The courtier shouts that it is an order of the Emperor that the heron be caught. The heron descends and bows low. The Emperor is pleased, and awards the fifth court rank to both the heron and the courtier. The heron dances in gratitude.

Sagi   Umewaka Kagefusa

Sesshôseki

Gennô, a priest, and his attendants are crossing Nasu Plain when they see a bird drop dead as it passes over a huge rock. They go toward the rock to investigate, and are stopped by a woman. She tells them that the rock is Princess Tamamo, who was actually a fox. She fell in love with the Emperor, but was sent away from his side. Her anger and frustration changed her into this rock. Any living being that approaches the rock dies immediately. The woman reveals that she is the spirit of the rock and vanishes into it.

Gennô and his attendants offer flowers and invocations. The rock splits in two and the fox appears. The fox dances in gratitude for the prayers which have destroyed its evil power and given its soul eternal salvation.

Sesshôseki Scene II
Teshima Yazaemon

Shakkyô Scene II   Shite: Kanze Hisao (left)
Tsure: Kanze Shizuo

Shakkyô

A priest goes to China to study and gain enlightenment.
When he reaches the foot of Mount Shôryô, and is about to cross
a narrow stone bridge which spans a deep ravine, he is stopped
by a woodcutter. The woodcutter tells the priest that this is the
bridge to a paradise and that he is not yet fit to cross it, but that
if he will wait, the servants of Saint Monju will come to
entertain him.

Presently two lion gods appear and dance among the red
and white peonies near the bridge.

Noh History and Theory

BACKGROUND

Noh is a highly stylized, masked song and dance drama, in which beauty of voice and movement are the highest aims. Comic vignettes called Kyôgen provide the comic relief between the heavier Noh plays. These two forms have developed side by side through the centuries and are collectively referred to as Nôgaku.

Noh themes and dramaturgy are extremely simple. The crecendo of a single emotion is presented by means of plastic form, spatial composition, and music. Subjects handled include filial piety, love, jealousy, revenge, and *samurai* spirit. The scripts often not only lack a coherent plot, but even purposefully avoid usual dramatic contrasts and development.

From the beginning of its history, Noh plays have always been written, composed and choreographed by the actors themselves. Over the several hundred years since their creation, the plays and the methods of presentation have been polished and improved by many generations of actors. In the repertoire are plays from before the time of Kan'ami (1333?-1384?) and his son Zeami (1364?-1443?), the perfectors of the art, their own works, plays written by their descendants during the 15th and 16th centuries, and a few which have been written during the last 100 years. Of course, because of the refining process which is still being carried out, the old plays are not presented in the exact manner or style of the time they were written.

Some of the individual characteristics of this operatic dance drama include; its unique stage, its complete concentration on the *shite* role, its use of masks, its use of dance as an important means of expression, its methods of vocalization, its highly poetic scripts, and its orchestra which is made up of a large hand drum (*ô-tsuzumi*), a small hand drum (*ko-tsuzumi*), a transverse flute (*fue*), and sometimes includes a stick drum (*taiko*).

THE NOH THEATRE

Noh is performed on a special stage which is quite different from the common procenium stage.

In ancient days, most performing arts were presented outdoors with the ground itself as a stage. Later on stages for the sacred Kagura dances appeared in shrines, where early Noh was also performed. Thus the Kagura stage was a strong influence in the subsequent development of the Noh theatre as we know it today.

The present style of stage is a copy of a theatre built by the Shogun in Edo Castle during the Tokugawa period. The original stage was built outdoors with the seating area for the audience in a separate building with an open area between. A stage of this type was built in 1881, and later moved to the grounds of Yasukuni Shrine in Tokyo where it stands today. Performances are still presented there with nature providing the sound and lighting effects.

Construction

Modern Noh theatres (*Nôgaku-dô*) are built with the stage and the seats for the audience under the same roof. However, the roof over the stage and the white gravel (*shirasu*) are still there as reminders of the origins of Noh. The white gravel spread on the ground between the stage and the audience in

Components of the Noh stage
Front view

1. *Age-maku* (lift-curtain)
2. *Hashi-gakari* (bridge-like extension)
3. *Ichi-no-matsu* (first pine)
4. *Ni-no-matsu* (second pine)
5. *San-no-matsu* (third pine)
6. *Kôken-bashira* (stage assistant's seat)
7. *Kagami-ita* (resounding board)
8. *A to-za* (up stage area behind the main stage)
9. *Fue-za* (flutist's seat)
10. *Ko-tsuzumi-za* (small hand drummer's seat)
11. *Ô-tsuzumi-za* (large hand drummer's seat)
12. *Taiko-za* (stick drummer's seat)
13. *Shite-bashira* (principal actor's pillar)
14. *Fue-bashira* (flutist's pillar)
15. *Jiutai-za* (chorus seating area)
16. *Waki-za* (secondary actor's seat)
17. *Waki-bashira* (secondary actor's pillar)
18. *Shirasu-bashigo* (steps crossing the white gravel)
19. *Metsuke-bashira* (pillar on which to fix the eyes)
20. *Shirasu* (white gravel)
21. *Kagami-no-ma* (greenroom)

the old outdoor theatres was for the purpose of reflecting the natural light of the sun to illuminate the stage.

The floor of the stage is unfinished Japanese cypress wood. The acting area is made up of four sections; the main stage, the up stage area behind the main stage called the *ato-za*, the porch-like area attached stage left called the *jiutai-za*, and the bridge-like structure leading off at an angle stage right of the *ato-za* called the *hashi-gakari*. At the end of the *hashi-gakari* behind the lift curtain (*age-maku*) is the greenroom or mirror-room (*kagami-no-ma*), and all across behind the whole stage area are the dressing rooms (*gaku-ya*).

The main stage protrudes out into the audience and its roof is supported by four wooden pillars. The total area of the main stage is approximately 30 square meters. The floor boards are laid from front to back and are highly polished to facilitate the sliding action of the performers' feet.

The *ato-za* is about 3 meters wide and runs all the way across the back of the main stage. The orchestra (*hayashi-kata*) sits in a line across the front of the *ato-za*. Reading from stage left to stage right is the flutist (*fue-kata*), the small hand-drummer (*ko-tsuzumi-kata*), the large hand-drummer (*ô-tsuzumi-kata*), and the stick drummer (*taiko-kata*). The floor boards of the *ato-za* run longways – perpendicular to those of the main stage.

On stage left is a porch-like protrusion (*jiutai-za*) where the chorus (*jiutai-kata*) sits in two neat rows. The usual number of singers is six to eight but is sometimes increased to ten.

Leading off at an oblique angle from the stage right end of the *ato-za* is the bridge-like *hashi-gakari*. At the end of the *hashi-gakari* is the lift-curtain (*age-maku*) through which the performers enter and leave the stage. There is no other curtain on the Noh stage, so if the performer ends the play in the center of the main stage, he must turn and walk quietly, in character, all along the *hashi-gakari* and through the *age-maku* before he is hidden from view. The *hashi-gakari* is considered, not just a simple passage-way, but an extension of the stage, and is often used most effectively as an additional acting area.

The only scenery is the wall behind the *ato-za* on which is painted an ancient pine tree. It is called the *kagami-ita* (literally, "mirror board" or, perhaps more logically, "resounding board"). All plays are performed before this single "back drop" — no other scenery as such is used. Its significance is more in terms of a religious, traditional part of the Noh stage itself than as actual background scenery for the Noh and Kyôgen plays. The *kagami-ita* contributes greatly to the strong, massive effect of the empty Noh stage itself. Thus, practically speaking, Noh and Kyôgen are danced, sung, and acted on a completely empty, scenery-less stage.

The wall at the stage left end of the *ato-za* is called the *waki-kagami-ita* (literally, "side resounding board"), and is decorated with a painting of young bamboo trees. In its lower left corner is a small sliding door called the *kirido-guchi*. The chorus and stage-assistants (*kôken*) enter and leave the stage through this door. Minor characters in Noh and Kyôgen also sometimes exit through the *kirido-guchi*, but never use it to make an entrance on the stage.

Since the square stage protrudes out into the audience, performances can be viewed from both the front and the side. For this reason the performer must gauge his acting to be effective not only in height and width, but also in depth. Noh has had, for hundreds of years, elements of such modern innovations as the "open stage" and "theatre-in-the-round."

The down stage right pillar is called the *metsuke-bashira* (literally, "the pillar on which to fix the eyes"). Its name comes from the fact that it is actually used by the main actor (*shite*) to determine his position on the stage since he has only extremely narrow eye holes in his mask. From the viewpoint of the audience, the *metsuke-bashira* gives a solidity to the cubical space of the stage, a three-dimensional sculptural effect to the movements and poses of the performer, and adds a strong sense of perspective to his down-up stage progress. In recent years, there has been some talk of taking away the *metsuke-bashira* in order to allow the audience a full view of the stage at all times, but without it, the special effect of Noh described above would be completely destroyed.

The length of the *hashi-gakari* is not absolutely set. The stage in Edo Castle, on which modern stages are modeled, is said to have had a seventeen-meter long *hashi-gakari*, but most of those today are considerably shorter. The *hashi-gakari* is not exactly perpendicular to the stage, but goes off at a wide oblique angle. Historical records indicate that *hashi-gakari* on early Noh stages led directly back in a straight line from up stage center. The angle was gradually diminished until the *hashi-gakari* finally reached its present position toward the end of the 16th century.

The pillar located up stage right at the point where the *hashi-gakari* joins the main stage is called the *shite-bashira*, because this is the point on the stage where the leading actor (*shite*) stops and announces his name – in other words, it is the point where the action of the play begins. Also throughout the play, the *shite* constantly returns to this position after every action, circuit of the stage, or series of dance movements – it is sort of his "home-base."

For similar reasons the pillar located down stage left in front of the *jiutai-za* is called the *waki-bashira*. The actor of the secondary role called the *waki* takes his position here, and always returns to this area.

Since the up stage left pillar is next to the flutist's seat, it is called the *fue-bashira* (literally, "flute pillar"). On the lower part of the *fue-bashira* is attached a large iron ring. The ring is used to secure the rope, which goes through a pulley in the center of the ceiling of the stage, to hold up the bell in *Dôjôji* (pps. 52-53). It is never used for any other purpose or in any other play.

The floor of the stage is raised a little less than one meter off the ground, and is very slightly raked, the *ato-za* and *jiutai-za* are absolutely horizontal, and the *hashi-gakari* forms a slight inclined plane from the *age-maku* up to where it connects with the main stage.

A knee-high railing extends across the back of the *jiutai-za* from the *waki-bashira* all the way up stage. Similar railings extend all the way along both sides of the *hashi-gakari*. Three small pine trees are planted at regular intervals in the white gravel (*shirasu*) in front of the *hashi-gakari*. These are called (beginning with the one nearest the main stage) *ichi-no-matsu* (first pine), *ni-no-matsu* (second pine), and *san-no-matsu* (third pine). These pines are one more reminder that Noh was originally performed outdoors. Acting on the *hashi-gakari* is always performed behind one or the other of the three pines. Thus they are very important guideposts in the staging of a Noh play.

The *age-maku* is made of five differently colored strips of damask sewn together lengthwise. It is lifted by two long bamboo poles which are attached to its bottom corners. Two stage assistants (*kôken*) sit on the floor of the greenroom, and raise and lower the curtain to facilitate the entrances and exits of the actors. The speed and rhythm by which the curtain is raised and lowered are important factors in creating the mood and setting the scene of a play in the imagination of both the audience and the performer. The musicians and stage assistants enter by slightly pulling open the up stage side of the *age-maku*.

A small flight of three steps called the *shirasu-bashigo* leads down into the audience from the down stage center edge of the stage. In the past, the official in charge of the temple or shrine at which a Noh performance was presented would enter the stage by means of these steps to announce the opening and closing of a program. Also servants of generals and other high ranking warriors would use these steps to convey gifts from their masters to actors on the stage. However, today the stairs serve no practical purpose – they have become nothing more than a part of the traditional design of the stage.

In the greenroom (*kagami-no-ma*) is a large mirror for the actor to contemplate his appearance while waiting for his entrance cue. There is also a small window (*arashi-mado*) through which both the stage and the audience can be viewed, in the wall of the greenroom.

Before the actor enters the greenroom, he is dressed by fellow actors in the costume and wig for his role. After sitting in front of the mirror for a few minutes, he ceremoniously receives the mask, and bows to it in greeting before it is secured in place by a stage assistant. This is a custom handed down from the days when masks were only used in religious ceremonies, and were thought to house the very soul of the god they represented.

Now in complete costume, the actor stands facing the

lift-curtain and whispers, "curtain" (*o-maku*), upon which the curtain is raised and he makes a perfectly timed entrance.

Lighting

In the past, lighting was provided by the natural light of the sun during the day, and by bonfires or candles at night. Electric lights were installed in a Noh theatre for the first time in 1894. The plan was pushed through by Kita Roppeita and Kanze Kiyoyasu against the bitter objections of the older actors Umewaka Minoru and Hôshô Kurô. At first naked light bulbs were placed in the four corners of the stage and in a few other places. There was a great deal of discussion about more artistic effects, but nothing was actually done till after the Second World War when all the theatres were rebuilt and florescent lights were installed. There was still a great deal of dissatisfaction because the new florescent lighting was too bright and completely changed the coloring of the masks and costumes. Improvements have been made and innovations have been tested, but a completely satisfactory lighting plan has yet to be discovered. In any case, Noh has come down to us through the centuries as an actor's art, always refusing to enlist the aid of external effects and decorations, therefore modern lighting effects, such as spot lights and colored illumination, go against the very nature of the art and should never be used under any circumstances.

Sound

Noh is music drama. Its music is made up of three elements; vocal (voices of the actors and the chorus), woodwind (the flute), and percussion (the drums). The angle of the ceiling is such that the sounds are amplified forward into the audience.

Large earthenware jars are buried under the floor boards of both the main stage and the *hashi-gakari* for the purpose of creating the special sound of the stamping of the actors' feet in the dances. The position of the jars and the angle at which they are buried has been a most heavily guarded secret of traditional Noh stage carpenters for many generations past. However, since the Second World War, a new method has been devised using concrete cones with sand in the bottom to produce the same effect. The resonance and tone are regulated by the amount of sand used. This new system seems to be quite effective and satisfactory.

Seating

The seating facilities of most early modern Noh theatres consisted almost entirely of cushions on a *tatami* mat floor, but chair-type seats gradually began to appear especially after the Second World War, until today almost all theatres have been converted to Western seating. However, cushions on *tatami* are still found at the back or on the second floor of even some of the most modernized Noh theatres in both Tokyo and Kyoto today.

In the past there was seating space on three sides of the stage, but now seats are installed only in front and around to the left of the stage in front of the *hashi-gakari*. The best seats are, of course, the first few rows across the front of the main stage from which the whole stage area as well as the full length of the *hashi-gakari* and the *age-maku* can be viewed comfortably. The seats in the fan shaped area (*naka-shômen*), between those facing straight front (*shômen*) and those directly facing the left side of the stage (*waki-shômen*), are the least expensive because the *metsuke-bashira* obstructs the view of all stage center action, however, seats in this area afford an excellent view of the secondary actor (*waki*) and the chorus. Many Noh connoisseurs prefer the direct side view of the actor afforded by the *waki-shômen* seats, because the movements of the *shite* actor can be studied at close range and the whole stage can be seen even when a large stage property is placed stage center.

THE NOH ACTOR

Noh is a highly stylized masked music drama centered around dance as its main element. Rather than concentration on plot development, its scripts present the building up and intensification of a single emotion or atmosphere through which the pursuit of beauty and truth is expressed. All aspects are severely simplified and refined to the highest possible degree resulting in a single strongly concentrated effect. This is an extremely Oriental and Japanese method of expression. The same basic concept is found in all traditional Japanese arts which were developed during the middle ages including tea ceremony, *ikebana, haiku* poetry, and *sumi-e* painting.

Noh does not require a large number of performers. Actually, the concentrated atmosphere is produced most effectively by a single performer in a single, simple, refined dance. However, at least one more actor is necessary to provide a motive for the dance — the foil on which deeper expression can be achieved. Thus Noh can be effectively performed with as few as two actors.

There are five separate schools in Noh — Kanze, Hôshô, Kita, Komparu, and Kongô. Each has slight differences in atmosphere, acting style, libretti, and use of masks and costumes. Kyôgen has two schools — Izumi and Okura. An actor is trained in and performs with the same school.

Shite and Waki

The main actor is called the *shite* and the secondary actor is called the *waki* in all Noh plays. As mentioned above, the role of the *waki* is merely for the purpose of calling the *shite* to the stage, to question him, and to provide the incentive for him to dance. The *waki* is always and ever in a secondary position, and as soon as he has accomplished his purpose, he retires to an unobtrusive position in a corner of the stage in order to direct the whole attention of the audience toward the performance of the *shite*. The same is true of all other roles which appear on the stage. This complete concentration on the *shite* role is the chief unique characteristic of Noh dramaturgy.

Sometimes the *shite* is accompanied by a servant, a friend, or a relative. These roles are called *tsure* (literally, "one brought along"), *tomo* (literally, "one in attendance"), and *kokata* (literally, "child," see section *kokata* on p. 111). There is also a stage assistant called a *kôken* who is responsible for keeping the *shite*'s costume in proper order, presenting hand props and additional costume parts to the *shite* at the proper time, and receiving them when the *shite* has finished using them. The chorus which provides the vocal accompaniment for the drama is also part of the *shite*'s group. All actors who take the above mentioned roles are referred to as "*shite* actors." The *waki* also sometimes has attendants or companions. These roles are all called *waki-zure* (literally, "brought along by the *waki*"). Each Noh actor is trained as either a *waki* or a *shite* actor and he spends his life acting roles only in his own field — in other words, a *waki* actor never performs a *shite* role and vice versa. This specialization results in an even greater contrast between the *shite* and *waki* on the stage than if they had been trained by the same teachers and according to exactly the same methods.

Masks and Roles

Waki roles fall into three distinct categories — Ministers (*daijin-waki*) including those on a mission for the Emperor and those in charge of important temples and shrines, Priests (*sô-waki*) including all ranks and religious sects, Common Men (*otoko-waki*) including warriors, townsmen, and villagers. The *waki* is always a human male who is alive at the time of the action of the play — he never represents a ghost, a demon, a god, or a woman.

The *waki*'s costume provides sufficient identification for his role, so his face is left bare, with no mask or make-up. He must make his role convincing through proper use of voice and gesture alone.

The *shite* is a different matter. He is required to portray any and all imaginable characters including old men, gods, mighty warriors, women, ghosts, and animals. There are numerous types of Noh, and since all plays center around the role of the *shite*, it naturally follows that the roles of the *shite* cover a broad range of characters. Thus many different types of costumes and masks are necessary. Not only in the case of non-human characters, but also when a full-grown man is required to play the part of a woman or a very old or very young man, it becomes necessary to hide or change his face in some way. In Kabuki and Peking Opera the problem is solved by the use of heavy make-up with a flat-white base. Noh solves the problem through the use of masks.

Masks are used as mentioned above for all non-human and female characters. Also many living human characters such as Shunkan and Kagekiyo require masks to show some special characteristic — for instance, Shunkan's extreme thinness and great disappointment, and Kagekiyo's advanced age and blindness. However, when the character is a healthy middle aged male, the *shite* actor appears with his own face, bare of any decoration. Plays of this type are called *hitamen-mono* (literally, "bare face plays") or *gendai-mono* (literally, "Present plays").

When a mask is not used, the actor makes every effort to keep his face completely immobile and expressionless even to the extent of not moving his eyes. Since the mask, and not the actor's face, is considered the essense of the character, when an actor does not use a mask, he thinks of his own face as taking the place of a mask. Different from other forms of drama, the humanity of the performer is concealed as much as possible in the attempt to express pure poetic "form" through his body and movements. The attempt to present a completely expressionless face at all times on the Noh stage is made by not only the unmasked *shite* actor, but by every person involved in the play including chorus, musicians, and stage assistants.

Kokata

Kokata means literally "child actor," and it indicates the type of role played by young boys around the age of ten. It is only natural that the roles of children should be acted by young actors, but there are also several adult roles which are taken by them in Noh. *Kokata* appear most often in the mad woman plays which depict a mother who has become temporarily deranged at the loss of her child, and regains her senses when they meet again either physically or through a vision of the spirit of the dead child as in *Sumidagawa* (p. 72).

Many times persons of very high rank, such as an Emperor, are played by *kokata*. This is done to take advantage of the innocence and purity of a child, and use him as a symbol of the character. Another reason is the constant attempt in Noh to concentrate all attention on the *shite*. If, for instance, an Emperor, who was a minor role in the play, were played realistically by an adult, it is only natural that the actor would attempt to express the dignity and power of his role, and this would unavoidably detract from the socially lower ranking character of the *shite*. For the same reason, the *kokata* is taught to speak his lines and move in a completely mechanical manner when playing this type of role. Examples of this are the roles of Emperor Kiyomibara in *Kuzu*, Yoritomo in *Daibutsu Kuyô*, and Yoshitsune in *Ataka* and *Funa Benkei*. The use of a *kokata* for Yoshitsune when he appears with Benkei is also for the purpose of stressing the physical size and strength of Benkei. Also when Yoshitsune and his lover Shizuka appear on the stage together, one or the other is played by a *kokata*. This is one more attempt to maintain the symbolic and the formal poetic aspect by detracting from the inherent sensuality in such a scene, which would come to the fore if both roles were played by adults. It is also one more example of the concentration on a single character in Noh dramaturgy.

Ai Kyôgen

There are both one and two scene Noh plays. In the two scene plays, the *shite* leaves the stage at the end of the first scene, changes his costume and reappears at the beginning of the second scene in some other form. The transition between the two scenes is the responsibility of a Kyôgen actor. He maintains the dramatic tension and atmosphere by explaining in simpler language the complicated Noh script, or performs a related or transitional scene of his own, sometimes in conversation with the *waki* and at other times alone. His role is called the *ai* (literally, "interval").

In the case of one scene plays, the *ai* often appears at the beginning of the piece, performs his part, and leaves the stage. In some plays, the *ai* becomes an integral part of the action as a retainer or assistant to the *shite* or *waki*, and is on the stage throughout the whole play. Kyôgen actors also provide comic relief between Noh plays with their delightful light vignettes which depict human beings at their most human.

TYPES OF NOH PLAYS

Recently evening performances of Noh have become popular. When a performance begins at five or six o'clock in the evening, it is not possible to present more than two Noh and one Kyôgen, and many performances consist of only one of each. Performances beginning late in the morning on Saturdays or Sundays often present three or four Noh with as many Kyôgen, but nowadays there are very few performances of the formal program which is made up of five Noh and four Kyôgen plays.

Noh plays are divided into five categories. The First Group is made up of God or Celebratory (*Waki Noh*) plays in which the *shite* is always a god, a demi-god, or the messenger of a god. The Second Group is made up of Ghost (*Shura Mono*) plays in which the *shite* is the ghost of a warrior of the Genji or Heike clans. The Third Group is made up of Woman or Wig (*Katsura Mono*) plays in which the *shite* is a beautiful woman. The Fourth Group is made up of miscellaneous subjects (*Zatsu Noh*), but since the best known of the group are those dealing with slightly deranged women, the whole group is commonly called Mad Woman (*Kyôjo Mono*) plays. The Fifth Group is made up of Demon (*Kichiku Mono*) plays in which the *shite* is a demon or devil. Kyôgen plays also follow the same general grouping, but there is a great deal more freedom in their use as part of one group or another.

The total Noh program as well as the single Noh play is built on the dramatic rhythm pattern called *jo-ha-kyû* (prelude-development-coda). Even when only two or three plays are presented on a program, this rhythm pattern is the basis for the choice of plays and their order in the program.

The *jo-ha-kyû* pattern was introduced into Noh from the ancient court dance called Bugaku. Zeami, the perfecter of Noh, stated in his writing on Noh theory five hundred years ago, "*Jo-ha-kyû* is found in every natural phenomenon and in every kind of art; let it be so in Sarugaku (old name for Noh) as well." (Zeami's *Kadensho* Chapter III Questions and Answers). *Jo-ha-kyû* is demanded not only as the overall rhythm for a program, but in each play, in each section of each play, and even in each phrase of the lyrics. It is the natural rhythm of all life. In the formal program of five Noh plays, the First Group play is the *jo*, the Second, Third, and Fourth group plays make up the three stages of development, forming the *ha*, and the Fifth Group play becomes the *kyû*.

Okina (p. 2) is a sacred ceremony which was performed in Japan long before the birth of Noh. It holds a special position among Noh plays and is presented only on special occasions such as New Years, memorial performances, and dedication services. It is performed before the First Group plays.

First Group

First Group God (*Waki Noh*) plays are of the two scene variety. The *shite* in the first scene tells a story or recites poetry concerning the origin of a temple or shrine. After the interval, he appears in the second scene as the god of the temple or shrine described in the first scene and performes a felicitous dance – *Takasago* (p. 9), *Ema* (p. 10), *Yôrô*, and *Yumi Yawata* are good examples. The photograph on page 8 shows the god in the second scene of *Takasago* dancing in front of orchestra members who are dressed in special hats called *samurai eboshi*, and brightly colored costumes. This special dress for the orchestra is used for First Group plays only when *Okina* is performed. In this case the orchestra does not leave the stage between *Okina* and the First Group play.

Second Group

The *shite* of all Second Group Ghost (*Shura Mono*) plays (except *Tomoe* (p. 21) which is about a female warrior and *Tamura* which is about a Shôgun) are warriors of the Genji-Heike clan battles who killed some famous enemy, died in battle, and have gone to hell. The ghost of the warrior tells a priest (the *waki*) the story of his last battle, and begs him to pray for his soul. Except for *Tamura, Yashima* (p. 16), and *Ebira*, all deal with warriors who fought on the losing side. The stories are taken from the classical battle chronicles "Tales of the Heike Clan" (*Heike Monogatari*) and "Chronicle of the Rise and Fall of the Genji and Heike Clans" (*Gempei Seisui Ki*). Examples of Second Group plays are *Sanemori* (p. 20), *Yorimasa* (p. 18), *Yashima* (p. 16), and *Atsumori* (p. 15).

Third Group

Third Group Wig (*Katsura Mono*) plays deal with beautiful women of the Heian Period (781-1189) most of whom appear in such classics as "Tales of Ise" (*Ise Monogatari*) and "The Tale of Genji" (*Genji Monogatari*). The stress is on melodies, gorgeous costumes, and graceful dances. Third Group plays are the center piece and artistic high point of a full Noh program. They are the most Noh-like – the most beautiful and elegant in all aspects. *Izutsu* (p. 25), *Matsukaze* (p. 32), *Yuya* (p. 33), *Eguchi* (p. 36), and *Hagoromo* (p. 44) are some of the better known plays of this group. *Oshio* and *Unrin'in* with the poet-aristocrat Ariwara Narihira (a man) as the *shite,* and *Bashô, Fuji, Yuki,* and *Kochô* with various spirits as their *shite* are exceptions to the rule in that the *shite* is not a woman. However, the delicacy of their poetry and the soft, feminine interpretation of the central character are the reasons for their inclusion in the Third Group.

Fourth Group

The Fourth Group includes plays handling a variety of subjects. Since they all deal with characters in some state of derangement or madness, the most typical and best known of which are those dealing with a mother who is crazed with grief at the loss of her child, they are commonly referred to as Mad Woman (*Kyôjo Mono*) plays. Another point, that most plays of this group have in common, is that their *shite* are all living human beings. There is more dramatic development and more actual movement on the stage than in other groups, therefore they are the easiest to follow and most interesting to watch. *Aoi-no-ue* (p. 50), *Dôjôji* (p. 52), Yoroboshi (p. 68), *Kagekiyo* (p. 79), *Ataka* (p. 80), and *Shunkan* (p. 82) are popular representatives of this group, most of which have been adapted as dance-dramas in Kabuki.

Fifth Group

The main characteristic of the Fifth Group Demon (*Kichiku Mono*) plays is their strong rhythm and fast tempo. Similar to the First Group God plays, the *shite* appears in human form in the first scene, then reveals his true form, that of a devil or a demon, in the second scene. Some plays handle good and others evil demons and devils. Those in which good demons appear, end in blessings for mankind. The evil demons are always conquered by a human being in the end. Popular plays of this group include *Kokaji* (p. 86), *Funa Benkei* (p. 88),

Kurozuka (or *Adachigahara*) depending on the school: (p. 92), and *Shakkyô* (p. 96).

The total repertoire including plays of all groups contains some 240 plays.

A formal Noh program covers the total range of the imagination – from gods, through all types of human beings, to demons – always ending with blessings and victory for mankind.

NOH COSTUMES

Masks

Noh, true to its designation as masked drama, requires a mask for the principle character in every play (excluding, that is, the special group of bare face plays described earlier). The mask is the very life-blood of Noh. The actors have an almost worshipful attitude of respect or awe in the presence of a mask. It is only after the actor has been completely dressed and has contemplated his own appearance in the mirror of the greenroom that he accepts the mask, lifts it up, bows his head in greeting, and has it secured on his face. Up to the time the mask is put on, the actor is still himself, but from the moment the mask is in place, he considers himself completely transformed into the character he is to portray. The actor is taught that he is not to put the mask on, but that he must put his whole self, body and soul, into the mask.

A few masks are used for only one specific role, but the bulk of them are general types such as beautiful woman, old man, and warrior. Different copies of the same mask all have only very slight differences — perhaps in coloring, texture, or general atmosphere. Even so, the particular copy of the mask to be used in a play for a given performance is very carefully chosen by the actor himself to fit his own personality and his interpretation of the role.

Masks are made of wood — usually Japanese cypress. First it is carved and then many layers of paint are added. To be a superior work, it must be both a masterpiece of carving and of painting. Many masks that have been passed down for generations over hundreds of years are great masterpieces of art. However, a mask can be fully appreciated only when it is brought to life by a great actor on the stage.

While Noh masks have a great dramatic effect, they also impose equally great limitations. It is said that the mask used determines the atmosphere and interpretation of a performance. This is true even of a different copy of the same mask as mentioned above. Except for the demon masks which show a strong expression, most Noh masks are completely expressionless — rather they have an "intermediate expression." Thus, expression of a definite emotion is the responsibility of the actor. It is the "intermediate expression" of the mask that gives the actor freedom to show delicate nuances of a broad range of emotional coloring.

A Noh actor often spends days contemplating the mask he plans to use for a single performance, choosing and rechoosing the costume he will use with it. The final ensemble is similar to a painting or a musical composition. Each part of the costume is chosen to contribute to the total effect and to enhance the *kurai* ("grade" or "rank") of the mask and harmonize with the *kurai* of the play.

The *zô-onna* (p. 39) mask is the face of a mature woman with an atmosphere of divine purity. It is used for goddesses and angels. The Hôshô school also uses it for beautiful women in Third Group wig plays, while the Kanze school uses *waka-onna* (p. 39), the Kongô school uses *magojirô*, and the Komparu and Kita school use *ko-omote*.

The *fukai* (p. 39) and *shakumi* masks are used for middle-aged women and mothers. These two masks look almost exactly alike, but the *fukai* has a city-bred intelligent atmosphere, while the *shakumi* seems more rustic and emotional.

The *deigan* (p. 54) mask is similar to the above, but it has gold eyes. It is used for beautiful middle-aged women possessed by jealousy such as Princess Rokujô in *Aoi-no-ue* Scene I (p. 50).

The *han'nya* (p. 54) mask with its horns and sharp fangs is probably the best known of all Noh masks. It expresses the fury of a woman turned demon by jealousy and frustration. It is used most effectively in Scene II of *Aoi-no-ue* (p. 51), *Dôjôji*, and *Kurozuka* (p. 93).

The *yamanba, uba, yase-onna,* and *rôjo* masks are used for roles of aged women.

The *shite* of almost all First Group God plays are old men for which the *ko-jô* (p. 11) mask is used. In Scene II of First Group God plays, such as *Takasago* and *Yumi Yawata,* the *kantan-otoko* mask is used. It was originally made for use in the play *Kantan* (p. 67), but its serene god-like appearance has resulted in its further use here.

The *shiwa-jô* (p. 11) and *ishi-ôjô* mask are used for dancing elderly man roles, the *warai-jô* and *asakura-jô* for lighter, happier old men, and the *aku-jô* (p. 11) for aged foreign gods in such plays as *Shirahige* and *Dômyôji,* as well as for angry or sorrowful ghosts of old men as in *Koi-no-Omoni* (p. 60) and *Aya-no-Tsuzumi.*

The *dôji* and *jidô* (p. 19) masks are used for ghosts of young men and youthful demi-gods such as the *shite* in Scene I of *Tamura* and *Kokaji* (p. 86) and Scene II of *Makura Jidô* (p. 65) and *Tenko* (p. 74). The *dôji* mask has a human-like face while the *jidô* is more elf-like. The *kasshiki* (p. 19) mask is used for roles of young lay-priests such as the *shite* in *Kagetsu,* and *Jinen Koji* (p. 69). Other young man masks such as *waka-otoko, ima-waka, Atsumori,* and *jûroku* are used for roles of young warriors.

The *heida* mask is used for most adult warrior roles such as the *shite* in *Yashima, Tamura, Ebira,* and *Kanehira.* The *chûjô* (p. 19) is used for adult aristocrats such as the *shite* in *Kiyotsune* (p. 14), *Tomonaga, Unrin'in, Tôru,* and *Oshio.*

The *yase-otoko* mask is used for ghosts of commoners such as fishermen in *Fujito* (p. 56) and *Akogi,* and the hunter in *Utou* (p. 62). Another mask of the same category is *kawazu* (p. 54) which shows the face of a drowned man.

The *ô-tobide* (p. 55) mask has a ferocious expression with eyes bulging and mouth wide open. It is used for roles of demons who move rapidly and violently such as the *shite* in Scene II of *Enoshima* and *Kuzu.* The *ko-beshimi* (p. 55) is used for sorrowful demons such as the *shite* in Scene II of *Nomori* and *Ukai.*

The *shishi-guchi* (literally, "lion's mouth"; p. 55) is used for the lion spirit in Scene II of *Shakkyô* (p. 96). It is from this play that all Kabuki lion dances are derived.

Two special masks are set aside for use only in *Okina* (p. 4). They are the *haku-shiki-jô* worn by the *shite* (p. 4) and the *koku-shiki-jô* worn by the Kyôgen actor for the role of *San-*

basô (p. 5). Both these masks, different from all other Noh masks, have the lower jaw carved as a separate piece and attached by strings at both sides. Also the eyebrows and beard are made of stiff hair and imbedded in the wood of the mask. Both have an expression of hearty laughter – the mouth spread wide and the eyes narrowed to slits.

Most of the highly prized masks are hundreds of years old. When one inspects them at close range, cracks, perpiration stains, discoloration, and warping are evident to the extent that the unpractised eye would find them almost ugly. However, viewed from the stage, it is these very masks that are the most artistically beautiful and have the most powerful dramatic effect.

Costumes

The common Japanese word for costume is *ishô,* but Noh costumes are referred to with the special term *shôzoku.* The Noh stage is undecorated and simple almost to the point of austerity, but in contrast the costumes, especially of the *shite* are gorgeous beyond description. They have been refined down through the centuries to become the highly stylized works of art – perfect in every detail of color, pattern, cut, and method of wearing – seen on the Noh stage today.

First the body of the actor is completely covered with pure white underwear and *tabi* socks. Next the plain silk garment is put on and the collar of the proper color to indicate the social rank of the character to be portrayed is attached. On top of this goes the gorgeous brocade kimono which has been carefully chosen by the actor for his interpretation of the role, then a harmonizing sash is tied in place around the waist. Finally an over-jacket, wide trouser-like *hakama,* a wig, and a headdress are put on depending on the requirements of the role.

The actor proceeds to the greenroom where he views himself in the mirror and receives the mask to complete his costume. A Noh connoisseur can tell, the minute an actor appears on the stage, how he intends to interpret the role, simply by the choice of the costume and mask and the manner in which he is wearing them.

NOH STAGE PROPERTIES

Noh has no set as such, but simple symbolic stage properties called *tsukuri-mono* (literally, "constructions") are used in the majority of the plays, which are constructed anew for each performance. Some scholars maintain that this is a custom dating back to the days when groups of Noh actors had to travel around the country to make a living, and were too poor to carry around large equipment, so they would construct their own stage properties each time they stopped to give a performance.

Hand properties such as fans, swords, and drums are made by specialized craftsmen. Some are fine works of art, and have been treasured and used for centuries as have many masks and costumes. They are generally referred to as *kodôgu* (literally, "small tools").

The largest of all the stage properties used on the Noh stage is the bell in *Dôjôji* (p. 53) which looks quite realistic though it is made of cloth spread over a bamboo frame with lead in the bottom edge to add weight. Most other stage properties are extremely simplified almost symbolic frames wrapped in cloth, that merely suggest a boat, a palanquin, a burial mound, or a thatched hut. Even so, they are very effective in creating the desired image. A particularly good example is the boat in *Funa Benkei* (p. 88). The frame is too small to hold all the actors who are supposed to be aboard, so some of them line up in front and back of the frame. But the viewer gets the impression that they are riding in the boat which is tossed about in the waves during the storm.

In *Eguchi* (p. 37), a decorative roof is added to indicate a pleasure boat, and in *Shunkan* (p. 82) a hawser is added to show that the boat is moored to a dock. On the other hand, in *Shichikiochi* two boats appear, but no stage property at all is used because they would only serve to clutter the stage. Also a boat frame is not used in *Sumidagawa* (p. 72) or *Jinen Koji* (p. 70) — the boatman simply uses a pole as though he is rowing a boat.

The palanquin in *Yuya* (p. 33) is quite unusual with its almost realistic roof and decorations of red ribbon. The effect is most realistic when *Yuya* peers out through the blinds at the cherry blossoms as she rides along, even though Munemori, who is, according to the script, riding along with her, actually walks along beside the decorated frame.

The mountain in *Yugyô Yanagi* (p. 34) and *Saigyô Zakura* (p. 35), as well as the burial mound in *Teika* (p. 46) and *Sumidagawa* (p. 72) are used to conceal a character who appears later, or for a character to disappear into during the course of the play. These stage properties consist of a tall square frame covered from top to bottom on three sides with a large cloth. In some cases the actor comes out from, or enters, through the rear. Other plays such as *Yôkihi* (p. 38) use a similar structure to represent a palace, or, as in *Kagekiyo*

(p. 79), a hut. In these plays, when the time comes for the *shite* to appear, the cloth is lowered to reveal him sitting inside.

The palace in *Yôkihi* is especially gorgeous with 36 brocade head bands hanging from the roof to represent a window blind. The pulling back of the blinds by mechanical means, as is seen in the photograph (p. 38) is an innovation introduced just before the Second World War by Kongô Iwao, which has now become common practice. Originally the *shite* pulled the blind back with his hand to peer out. This is just one example of the constant change found even in as strict a classical art as Noh. Many reforms are necessary and bring about definite improvements, but this particular one detracts from the mood of the play and should be done away with.

The work of the stage assistants (*kôken*), such as moving properties on and off the stage, helping an actor change his costume on stage, or retrieving hand properties, is very important in maintaining the mood and atmosphere of the play. They must know the play being performed as well or better than the *shite* himself, and must work smoothly, quickly, and unobtrusively. Thus these duties are traditionally performed by fellow actors of the *shite* — in some cases more experienced and of higher rank than the *shite* himself.

NOH DRAMATURGY

Noh is music-drama. Its lyrics are called *Yôkyoku* (literally, "song music"). Noh is danced to the accompaniment of the lyrics and the four piece orchestra. Strictly speaking, a Noh play is not "acted" but "danced," because it was originally developed from popular and religious songs and dances. Also because the dances in the piece and the movements that link them together should all be of a texture that shows no sharp uneven transitions. This is true whether the movement or gesture is explanatory semi-realistic mime or a purely symbolic one. Noh dance is not of the open leaping variety, but is a closed, controlled, sedate dance of the soul, closely related to the floor of the stage it is danced upon. In Japanese it is referred to as *mai* rather than *odori*, the more common word for dance. The distinction is inherent in these two words themselves.

The lyrics also have sung sections and spoken sections, but the spoken sections have an unique intonation pattern entirely unlike common dialogue. Thus Noh is different in every way from any other form of drama — it is more musical than musical comedy, but not as lyrically musical as opera, nor as conversational and realistic as a Western play. The total effect of Noh vocalization is closer to liturgy or Gregorian chant then anything else known to the Western world.

Kan'ami (1333?-1384?) wrote such plays as *Jinen Koji*, *Kayoi Komachi*, and *Sotoba Komachi*. His son Zeami (1364?-1443?) left numerous masterpieces. Zeami's son Motomasa (died 1432) wrote such popular plays as *Sumidagawa*, *Yoroboshi*, *Uta Uranai*, and *Morihisa*, even though he died at a very early age. Zeami's son-in-law Komparu Zenchiku (1405-1470?)

thus became head of the family and wrote numerous plays including *Ugetsu, Bashô,* and *Tamakazura.* Nobumitsu (1435-1516), the seventh son of Zeami's nephew On'ami, wrote plays full of action including *Ataka, Funa Benkei, Rashômon,* and *Chôryô.* However, these plays do not exist today exactly as they were written and performed during the lives of their creators.

The refinement of Noh into the beautiful, dignified art with a complete wedding of mime, song, and dance, and its further stylization, under the influence of warrior-like ethics and ideals, took place after Tokugawa Ieyasu became Shogun in 1603, and designated Noh as the official art of his government. This is basically the Noh we know today.

PHOTO PAGE INDEX

HOIKUSHA COLOR BOOKS
ENGLISH EDITIONS

Book Size 4″×6″

COLORED ILLUSTRATIONS FOR NATURALISTS

Text in Japanese, with index in Latin or English.

First Issues (Book Size 6″ × 8″)

Second Issues (Book Size 7″ × 10″)

Third Issues (Book Size 6″ × 8″)

< ENGLISH EDITIONS >

SHELLS
OF
THE
WESTERN
PACIFIC
IN
COLOR

Book Size 7″×10″

⟨vol. I⟩ by Tetsuaki Kira
(304 pages, 72 in color)
⟨vol. II⟩ by Tadashige Habe
(304 pages, 66 in color)

FISHES
OF
JAPAN
IN
COLOR

Book Size 7″×10″

by Toshiji Kamohara
(210 pages, 64 in color)